Original title:
Stitching Stars

Copyright © 2024 Creative Arts Management OÜ
All rights reserved.

Author: Natalia Harrington
ISBN HARDBACK: 978-9916-90-744-3
ISBN PAPERBACK: 978-9916-90-745-0

## **Tethered to the Cosmic Loom**

In the silence of the night, we gaze,
Stars like whispers, a cosmic maze.
Threads of fate in the sky unfold,
Tethered to dreams, both young and old.

Galaxies dance in a waltz of grace,
Each twinkle tells a timeless place.
A tapestry woven with love and fear,
In the loom of space, our paths are clear.

Light-years stretch, yet we feel so near,
Bound by the stardust, we have no fear.
Through endless nights, we search and yearn,
For the cosmic tales that twist and turn.

As shadows flicker, and comets sweep,
The universe holds the secrets we keep.
Tethered to brilliance, we drift and soar,
In the arms of the cosmos, forevermore.

## Constellation Weavers

We are the weavers of starlit threads,
Mapping the heavens where wonder spreads.
In a tapestry bright, we find our way,
Guided by constellations, night into day.

With each spark that ignites in the dark,
We stitch our hopes, a celestial arc.
Plans intertwined like the stars above,
In this cosmic dance, we share our love.

Every figure drawn tells a story rare,
Of heroes, dreams, and the things we dare.
Nebulas whisper, and the comets sing,
Creating a symphony of everything.

As night falls softly, we find our place,
Within the universe, full of grace.
Constellation weavers, hand in hand,
Crafting our destiny in stardust land.

## **Starry Fabrications**

In the night sky, dreams take flight,
With twinkling stars, a bright delight.
Whispers of tales, unspun and spun,
Crafting a world where shadows run.

Mirrored visions in cosmic streams,
Each wish ignites the silent beams.
Stories woven with starlit grace,
Moments captured in time and space.

## Emblems of the Cosmos

Galaxies swirl in a dance of light,
Emblems of wonder that shine so bright.
Constellations whisper ancient lore,
Mapping the skies, forevermore.

In every twinkle, a story lies,
Secrets hidden in the vast skies.
Planets align in a celestial game,
Calling our hearts, igniting the flame.

## **Night's Patchwork**

Stitched with darkness, the sky unfolds,
A patchwork of dreams, both new and old.
Sewed by the hands of time and fate,
Each piece a wonder, none too late.

Fleeting moments, like stitches blend,
Creating a canvas that will not end.
Threads of silver, woven with care,
A tapestry rich, beyond compare.

## **Celestial Embroidery**

In the fabric of night, stars entwine,
Celestial threads that softly shine.
Embroidered whispers in the silent air,
Tales of the cosmos, timeless and rare.

Every stitch a promise, every knot a dream,
Uniting the universe in a delicate seam.
With each dawn's light, the pattern renews,
A masterpiece painted in endless hues.

## **Celestial Threading**

Stars like needles, so fine and bright,
Stitching the fabric of endless night.
Galaxies swirl, a cosmic grace,
Each twinkling point, a sacred place.

Constellations weave a tale so grand,
Guiding dreamers with a gentle hand.
Through the shadows, a spark ignites,
Threads of wonder in starry sights.

## **The Tapestry of Night**

In the deep hues of twilight's wave,
Moonlight dances, soft and brave.
Whispers of the stars unfold,
Stories woven in silver and gold.

Night's cool breath, a velvet caress,
Cradles the world in tranquil rest.
Each shadow holds a secret bright,
In the tapestry spun by the night.

## **Weaving Light in Darkness**

Amidst the shadows, a beacon glows,
Hope's gentle touch as the cold wind blows.
Threads of courage, spun from the heart,
Binding us close when the world falls apart.

Fingers weaving with dreams and grace,
Creating a refuge, a warm embrace.
With every stitch, a tale unfolds,
Of light emerging, resilient and bold.

## **Moonlit Embroidery**

Under the moon's soft, watchful gaze,
Nature unfurls in delicate ways.
Stitches of silver on a canvas wide,
Flora and fauna in harmony abide.

Each petal blooms with luminescent light,
Woven with care through the quiet night.
In the night's embroidery, beauty stays,
A tranquil reminder of love's quiet ways.

## **Luminous Creations**

In the stillness of night,
Stars whisper secrets bright,
Crafted from cosmic dust,
A tapestry of trust.

Every flicker, a spark,
Guiding dreams from the dark,
They dance in silent glee,
Painting tales we can't see.

With colors bold and clear,
Each hue, a silent cheer,
Luminous hearts unfold,
In mysteries untold.

They shimmer on the sea,
Like thoughts, wild and free,
A song of light resounds,
In creations where hope abounds.

## Spun from Light

Threads of hope interlace,
In the heart of space,
Sunbeams weave and twine,
In patterns so divine.

Gentle whispers arise,
From the depths of the skies,
Carried on silver rays,
They guide us through our days.

Each moment, crafted fine,
A blend of yours and mine,
Spun from light's embrace,
Transforming every place.

In the warmth of dawn's hue,
New beginnings break through,
We wander, hand in hand,
On this luminous strand.

## Fabric of Unseen Dreams

Woven threads of desire,
Ignite a hidden fire,
In shadows softly creep,
The dreams we dare to keep.

Every stitch tells a tale,
Of journeys vast and frail,
In silence, they awake,
The courage we might take.

Layers deep, they reside,
Where hope and fears collide,
With gentle care, we stitch,
The fabric of our wish.

As night begins to fade,
New dawns are thus portrayed,
Unseen dreams take their flight,
To greet the morning light.

**Cosmic Patterns Unfurled**

In the dance of the stars,
Echoes near and far,
Galaxies spin and swirl,
In cosmic patterns, twirl.

Each heartbeat sings a tune,
Beneath the watchful moon,
While comets paint the night,
With trails of purest light.

Time flows, unbound and free,
Like the vast, endless sea,
Where mysteries align,
In the grand design.

The universe unfolds,
Stories yet untold,
In the spiral embrace,
Of this celestial space.

## Twilight Needlepoint

In twilight's glow, the threads entwine,
With shades of blue and soft, divine.
A needle dances, swift and bright,
Stitching dreams in fading light.

Whispers of stars beckon above,
A tapestry of night, stitched with love.
Each thread a story, brightly spun,
Underneath the setting sun.

### The Divine Darn

In hands that weave the fabric fine,
A rip repaired, with love's design.
Each careful stitch a prayer implored,
A garment mended, peace restored.

The needle glides, creation sings,
A dance of thread, as hope takes wings.
In certain hands, the flaws are art,
A patchwork tale, a loving heart.

## Crafting Celestial Wonders

Beneath the skies, with needle's grace,
We stitch the stars in endless space.
A quilt of moons, so bright and rare,
Celestial wonders, crafted with care.

The cosmos calls, we heed the sound,
Each stitch a journey, heaven-bound.
With every thread, a tale unfolds,
Of ancient nights and dreams of gold.

## **Tying the Heavens**

With finger's touch, the heavens tie,
In patterns spun from earth and sky.
Through threads of light, our spirits soar,
Weaving worlds forevermore.

A tapestry of fate, so grand,
Intertwined, each life we stand.
In every knot, a bond is cast,
Together stitched, our lives are vast.

## **Ethereal Woven Dreams**

In the silence, shadows dance,
Whispers echo, a fleeting chance.
Starlit threads in twilight gleam,
Weaving softly, an ethereal dream.

Through the mist where secrets hide,
Hearts unbound in twilight's tide.
With every breath, a story spun,
In woven dreams, we feel as one.

## **The Night's Canvas**

A canvas stretched across the skies,
With stars like paint, the darkness lies.
Brushstrokes of silver, whispers of light,
In the night's embrace, we take flight.

The moon spills gold on fields below,
Where shadows and light in harmony flow.
A masterpiece of calm and fear,
On the night's canvas, we draw near.

## A Stitch in the Milky Way

Each star a stitch in endless space,
A constellation's warm embrace.
Threads of light, both bold and faint,
Through the cosmos, dreams we paint.

In the galaxy's gentle sway,
We find our whispers, lost and stray.
A tapestry of hope and fear,
Each stitch a memory, crystal clear.

## Stellar Tapestry

Woven dreams in the night sky,
Threads of stardust, drifting high.
Patterns form in silence deep,
Guarding secrets that we keep.

Galaxies twirl in graceful embrace,
Where time and space find their place.
In this stellar tapestry so vast,
Weaving futures, learning from the past.

## Night's Luminous Mosaic

Stars strewn across the dark,
A celestial canvas glows,
Whispers of ancient tales,
In the silence, a story flows.

Moonlight drapes the quiet earth,
Casting shadows on the ground,
Each glimmer a fleeting spark,
In the night's embrace, we're bound.

Dreams take flight on silver beams,
Guided by the cosmic dance,
While the world gently sleeps on,
In this wondrous, timeless trance.

Eternal secrets linger here,
In the cool of midnight air,
Night's mosaic, vast and bright,
A beauty beyond compare.

## Cosmic Threads Unraveled

In the tapestry of space,
Threads of light intertwine,
Weaving stories of the stars,
In patterns so divine.

Time unfurls like a ribbon,
As galaxies swirl and fade,
Each moment a precious gem,
In the grand design displayed.

Echoes of the universe,
Whisper secrets in the dark,
Cosmic threads connect us all,
In the silence, hear their spark.

As we gaze into the night,
We embrace the endless flow,
In the heart of this vastness,
We find a home, a glow.

# Patterns of the Infinite

Waves of energy collide,
In the void where dreams reside,
Fractals form and shift with grace,
Infinite realms we can trace.

The dance of atoms sings aloud,
In patterns intricate and proud,
Each movement a symphony,
Of nature's vast geometry.

Galaxies spiral like a shell,
In the dark, they weave and dwell,
Threads of life and time entwined,
A universe so well designed.

Through the cosmos we shall soar,
Unraveling the endless lore,
In the patterns of the night,
We find our spark, our guiding light.

## **Handcrafted Heavens**

Clouds stitched from silver threads,
Skies painted in hues of blue,
Sunrise brings a gentle warmth,
A masterpiece born anew.

Mountains rise like silent guards,
Their peaks adorned with light,
Nature crafts her art with care,
In both shadow and in bright.

Rivers carve the earth with grace,
Flowing in a dreamy trance,
Every bend a brushstroke laid,
In a timeless, fluid dance.

Handcrafted heavens whisper low,
Stories from the stars above,
In the beauty we behold,
We find the essence of love.

## The Embroidered Sky

Stars twinkle like gems,
In a velvet embrace,
A tapestry woven,
By time's gentle grace.

Whispers of twilight,
Softly they sigh,
Painting the heavens,
With colors that fly.

Clouds drift like shadows,
In the moon's golden glow,
Threads of silver light,
In the night's quiet flow.

As dawn starts to break,
The stitches unwind,
A new day is born,
With secrets to find.

## Astral Weavings

Galaxies spin slowly,
In the cosmic sea,
Each thread a story,
That's waiting to be.

Nebulas form softly,
Like dreams in the night,
A quilt of existence,
Bathed in starlight.

The comets they dance,
In a wild serenade,
Sewing the heavens,
In hues that won't fade.

A tapestry unfolds,
As the planets align,
In this vast universe,
Our hearts intertwine.

## Night's Fabric of Fate

Under the blanket dark,
The stars find their place,
Weaving our destinies,
With every embrace.

The moon whispers secrets,
To lovers at night,
Crafting dreams softly,
In luminous light.

Each shadow signifies,
Paths yet to explore,
A fabric of moments,
With tales to implore.

In the silence we hear,
The hopes that await,
Threads of our journey,
In night's fabric of fate.

## **Crafting Light's Patterns**

Sunrise paints the dawn,
With colors so bright,
Crafting patterns of hope,
In the soft morning light.

Breezes hum a tune,
As blossoms unfold,
Each petal a promise,
Of stories retold.

The canvas of day,
Is a masterpiece true,
Each moment a stitch,
In the grand view.

As the stars take their place,
In the deepening blue,
We find magic in light,
In patterns anew.

# Celestial Threads

In the night sky, stars align,
Threads of silver, a design.
Whispers of the cosmic art,
Binding worlds, heart to heart.

Galaxies in gentle sway,
Each a story in display.
Woven tales of light and time,
In this fabric, dreams can climb.

Nebulas bloom, colors bright,
Painting darkness with their light.
In the cosmos' vast embrace,
We find our home, our rightful place.

As the universe unfolds,
Tales of old, yet to be told.
Celestial threads, intertwined,
In every heart, a spark defined.

## Tapestry of Night

The moon hangs low, a silver glint,
In shadows deep, where dreams hint.
Stars like beads on fabric strung,
In the quiet, our hearts are sung.

Clouds drift by in soft, slow dance,
Weaving magic with each glance.
Night's embrace, a velvet sheet,
In the stillness, souls meet sweet.

The whispers of the gentle breeze,
Carry secrets through the trees.
In the darkness, beauty found,
Tapestry of night astound.

Underneath this vast expanse,
Every twinkle, a fleeting chance.
To lose ourselves, to drift away,
In the night's sweet, soft ballet.

## **Weaving Dreams in the Sky**

Beneath the stars where wishes flow,
Weaving dreams with every glow.
Threads of hope in colors bright,
Stitching wishes in the night.

Clouds like canvas, drift and turn,
In the heart, a new fire burns.
Skies ablaze with every thought,
In this moment, joy is caught.

Crickets sing their lullaby,
As we weave dreams in the sky.
With every stitch, our spirits rise,
In this world, we find our ties.

Together we can paint the dawn,
With dreams spun pure, like a fawn.
In the tapestry of the night,
We weave our dreams, in love's light.

## **Embroidered Constellations**

In midnight's cloak, the stars awake,
Embroidered skies, no heart can break.
Each constellation tells a tale,
Of ancient paths, across the veil.

Stitched in silver, lines of fate,
Drawn together, never late.
In this fabric vast and wide,
We find our truth, our dreams abide.

Galaxies spin, a dance so grand,
A cosmic quilt, by love's own hand.
In each spark, our wishes soar,
Embroidered constellations, forevermore.

With every glance, a story told,
Of hopes and dreams and hearts so bold.
In this tapestry, let's abide,
As the universe flows, side by side.

## **Midnight Creations**

In the quiet hush of night,
Whispers of dreams take flight.
Stars dance on velvet skies,
Painting secrets, oh so shy.

Moonlight spills on silver streams,
Woven from the fabric of dreams.
Each shadow tells a tale,
Of forgotten worlds, pale and frail.

Creatures stir, both strange and bright,
In the depths of soft twilight.
Hope glimmers, twinkling wide,
In a heart where wonders hide.

A tapestry of night unfolds,
With stories waiting to be told.
Midnight's brush, so deft and keen,
Paints the edge of what has been.

## **Galaxies in a Seam**

Threads of stars, a cosmic line,
Stitching dreams with patterns fine.
In a quilt of time and space,
Galaxies form, each finds its place.

Nebulas swirl in vibrant hues,
Whispers of ancient cosmic news.
Each stitch a spark of light,
In the seam of endless night.

Planets spin in rhythmic song,
In the fabric, they belong.
Celestial seams that bind and weave,
In the universe, we believe.

Faint echoes of a distant sound,
In this intertwining, we are found.
Galaxies twirl, forever free,
In the patchwork of eternity.

## Celestial Couture

In the workshop of the skies,
Stardust tailors, wise and wise.
Dresses made of comet tails,
Sewn with light, where beauty trails.

Moon beams drape like silken folds,
Worn by night, as darkness molds.
Each gown a glimpse of night's embrace,
Fashioned with celestial grace.

Stars adorn the neckline bright,
Twinkling gems in velvet night.
With every stitch, the heavens sing,
In cosmic threads, the night takes wing.

Couture crafted from dreams afire,
Cloth of hope, we all desire.
In the fabric of the sky,
We wear the dreams that never die.

## Radiant Fabrications

In the forge where starlight gleams,
Radiant fabrications weave dreams.
Threads of gold and silver hues,
Crafting tales, a cosmic muse.

The loom spins tales of distant lands,
Where fate is stitched by skilled hands.
Galaxies flare, a vibrant show,
In the patterns that ebb and flow.

Nebula's heart forms gentle seams,
Woven tightly with whispered dreams.
Each creation, a spark divine,
In the night's grand design.

With each thread, the cosmos sighs,
As radiant visions fill the skies.
In the fabric of myth and lore,
We find the dreams we can explore.

## Fabric of the Universe

In the loom of night, we weave,
Cosmic threads that interleave.
Stars in patterns brightly shine,
A tapestry by design.

Waves of light in colors blend,
Through the dark, they twist and bend.
Galaxies in swirling dance,
Every note a vast expanse.

Planets spin on silver thread,
In the silence, secrets spread.
Whispers from the distant past,
In this fabric, shadows cast.

Hearts aligned with every beat,
In the cosmos, love is sweet.
Together in this quilt we find,
The universe, our hearts entwined.

## Starry Weaves and Moonlit Knots

Underneath the starlit skies,
We find magic in our eyes.
Moonlit knots of silver glow,
Binding dreams that ebb and flow.

Threads of stardust softly hum,
In the night, their voices come.
Weaving tales both far and near,
Echoes of the night we hear.

Tangled in the cosmic thread,
Every word and thought we've said.
Stories that the heavens hold,
In our hearts, the stars unfold.

As the night wraps us so tight,
We embrace infinity's light.
Starry weaves and moonlit knots,
In this moment, time forgot.

## Threads of the Milky Way

Across the vast, the stars align,
Threads of fate, a grand design.
Winding through this endless space,
Each connection finds its place.

Glistening like a river wide,
In the dark, our hopes confide.
Wisps of light that softly glide,
Charting paths where dreams collide.

Galactic chords that gently play,
Melodies of the Milky Way.
In each note, the universe sings,
Life's sweet dance, the joy it brings.

Through the threads that intertwine,
In this vastness, you are mine.
Together through the heavens sway,
Hand in hand, we find our way.

## **Celestial Needlework**

With stardust in the seams we mend,
Cosmic stories that never end.
Stitches made from light and space,
Creating beauty with each trace.

Stars like beads on velvet dark,
Embroider tales that leave a mark.
In this craft of dreams and light,
We design the endless night.

Needles dance with comets' tails,
Through the cosmos, our love sails.
Every thread a wish bestowed,
In the fabric, love's abode.

Celestial art that binds us tight,
In the twilight, hearts ignite.
In the needlework of fate,
Together, we will navigate.

## Woven Whispers of Light

In twilight's soft embrace, they gleam,
Threads of gold through shadows stream.
Whispers dance on gentle air,
   Carried forth by secret fare.

With every flicker, tales unfold,
Of love and loss, of brave and bold.
Stars align in silent vow,
   Guiding hearts in present now.

Sewn within the fabric fine,
Glimmers of the divine twine.
Softly they hum, the songs of night,
   Woven whispers, pure delight.

As dawn approaches, shadows flee,
   Threads of hope weave destiny.
In every heart, a spark ignites,
   Woven whispers of soft light.

## **Dreams in the Cosmic Loom**

In the loom where starlight gleams,
We weave together all our dreams.
Galaxies twirl in endless flight,
Stitched by the hand of cosmic might.

Nebulas bloom with colors bright,
A tapestry spun of pure delight.
Each thread a wish, each knot a sigh,
Echoes of hope that never die.

In midnight's hush, we find our place,
Embraced by time, wrapped in space.
Dreams intertwine, forever sewn,
In the fabric of the unknown.

As dawn breaks through, an artful seam,
We cherish the threads, the heart's bright beam.
In every heart, a story weaves,
Dreams in the cosmic loom, it leaves.

## **Celestial Knots**

Tied with care in the night's dark seam,
Celestial knots stitch each fleeting dream.
Woven high in the skies so vast,
Each twinkling light, a memory cast.

With lunar tales in whispers told,
Stars embrace the night so bold.
A tapestry of fate and time,
In the cosmos, a silent rhyme.

Knots of love, of loss, of grace,
Bound together in endless space.
Each gentle twist a life portrayed,
In celestial threads, we are laid.

As the morning sun breaks through the dark,
A brand new day, a vibrant spark.
Celestial knots, our hearts ensnare,
In the dance of life, forever rare.

## Aurora's Fabric

Beneath the dome where colors merge,
Aurora's fabric starts to surge.
Threads of emerald, gold, and rose,
Set the canvas, the heavens compose.

In swirling dance, the night ignites,
Whispers of magic, celestial lights.
Weaving tales of the earth's delight,
Stitching shadows in the dawn's soft light.

A quilt of wonder, bright and bold,
Stories of ages in hues unfold.
Bound by the skies, a joyous flare,
Aurora's fabric, beyond compare.

In every moment, each brushstroke shines,
Reflecting dreams across the lines.
As night gives way to morning's grace,
Aurora's fabric finds its place.

## Interstellar Stitchery

In the silence of the night,
Stars weave tales in silver light.
Threads of nebulae twist and twine,
Crafting dreams that softly shine.

Galaxies dance in cosmic seams,
Sewing visions, sparking dreams.
Every stitch a story told,
In the fabric of the bold.

Fingers trace the Milky Way,
In patterns that the shadows play.
A tapestry of hope unfolds,
In shimmering threads of gold.

Among the void, they stitch anew,
Creating worlds in shades of blue.
Interstellar threads unite,
In a fabric bound by light.

## **Skybound Creations**

Clouds above, a canvas wide,
Nature's brush, a gentle guide.
Rainbows arc with colors bright,
Skybound wonders, pure delight.

Birds on wings, they soar and dive,
Crafting journeys, feeling alive.
Whispers of the winds they chase,
In the infinite, they find their place.

Stars at dusk begin to gleam,
In twilight's heart, they softly dream.
Every flicker, a wish in flight,
Creating magic in the night.

Beneath the vast and endless dome,
We find ourselves, we call it home.
In the canvas, bold and free,
Skybound creations, meant to be.

## The Universe's Quilt

Galaxies woven, a grand design,
Stardust patterns, interline.
Each patch holds a tale profound,
In the silence, secrets found.

Constellations stretch and gleam,
Stitched together, a cosmic dream.
Colors swirling, light and shade,
In the quilt, the night parade.

Celestial thread, a tapestry,
Binding space and time with glee.
Every star, a shimmering place,
In the fabric of the endless space.

Eternity wraps us in its fold,
Stories of the brave and bold.
In the cosmic warmth we dwell,
In the universe's quilt, we spell.

## Cosmic Couture

Draped in starlight, the night's attire,
Galactical threads set hearts afire.
Nebulae lace the fabric fine,
In cosmic couture, we intertwine.

Sewing dreams with threads of gold,
Fashioned by stories, ancient and bold.
Moonbeams flash in elegance rare,
Our essence woven in stardust air.

From the dark, the fabric gleams,
As celestial fashion fuels our dreams.
Each star a jewel that shimmers bright,
In cosmic couture, we take flight.

With every seam, new worlds are spun,
Threads of fate, a journey begun.
In the night's embrace, we twirl and sway,
In cosmic couture, forever we play.

## Astronomical Artistry

Beneath the starry sky, we gaze,
Where constellations dance and blaze.
With brushes dipped in cosmic light,
We paint our dreams in the starry night.

Galaxies swirl in vibrant hues,
Celestial wonders, vast and true.
Each twinkling star a spark of hope,
In this vast canvas, we learn to cope.

Nebulas bloom like flowers bright,
In the universe's boundless sight.
Our hearts beat in rhythm with the stars,
Connecting us, no matter how far.

In this astronomical art we find,
The threads of magic woven in kind.
For every wish cast into the night,
Is a part of us, a guiding light.

## The Fabric of Wishes

Woven dreams on threads of gold,
Stories of wishes yet untold.
Every stitch a hope, a prayer,
Crafting futures from thin air.

In the loom of fate, we intertwine,
Each desire in designs divine.
Patterns form with threads of fate,
In the quiet, we create.

Tangled knots and frayed ends,
In this fabric, love transcends.
As we stitch the night with care,
We bind our dreams in the air.

With every knot, a spark ignites,
In the tapestry of starry nights.
Our hearts, a quilt, forever stitched,
In the fabric of wishes, souls enriched.

## **Lunar Needlecraft**

By the moon's soft, silvery light,
We craft our dreams into the night.
With needles sharp and threads so fine,
We sew our aspirations, line by line.

Each stitch a whisper of the heart,
In the needlecraft, we play our part.
Moonbeams glide on fabric spun,
An art of shadows, a dance begun.

Lunar secrets in patterns flow,
In twilight's glow, our spirits grow.
With every twirl, a hope takes flight,
In the lunar needlecraft, we unite.

As we thread our wishes, pure and bright,
The cosmos watches over, a guiding light.
In every loop, our dreams are cast,
In a tapestry of nights, we hold steadfast.

# **Cosmic Kreations**

From stardust born, our dreams take shape,
In cosmic colors, no escape.
Galactic strokes in infinite hue,
Creating worlds both old and new.

With cosmic hands, we mold the stars,
Crafting beauty from afar.
Every heartbeat, a celestial sway,
In the cosmic kreations, we find our way.

Planets spin on a canvas vast,
Time and space forever cast.
In the depths of the universe's heart,
We weave together, never apart.

So lift your gaze to the night sky wide,
In the cosmic realm, let dreams abide.
For every sparkle, a story true,
In cosmic creations, there's me and you.

## **Crafting Dreams in the Sky**

Beneath the azure canvas wide,
I sketch my hopes with stars as guide.
Each thought a feather, light and free,
I weave my wishes, you and me.

With every cloud, a whispered tale,
A fleeting breeze, a gentle sail.
The sun dips low, my heart ignites,
In twilight's glow, my soul takes flight.

I pen my dreams with silver threads,
In dusk's embrace, where magic spreads.
Each night a tapestry unfolds,
A story spun in starlit folds.

Crafting dreams in the sky so vast,
Where futures bloom and shadows cast.
In every star, I find my place,
A dance of hope in cosmic space.

## Galaxy Quilt

Stars aligned in patterns bright,
Forming seams of pure delight.
A quilt of galaxies unfold,
In midnight's grasp, a tale is told.

Celestial patches, dark and light,
Every corner, a world in sight.
Nebulas swirl in colors bold,
A cosmic fabric, dreams we hold.

In stitched connections, we explore,
Crafting memories forevermore.
With each small patch, we stitch our fate,
A galaxy quilt, we celebrate.

Beneath the stars, we find our thread,
In cosmic warmth, no fear or dread.
We fold the night, a tale to tell,
In this quilted sky, we dwell.

## Twinkling Patterns

In the stillness of the night,
Stars weave tales of pure delight.
Twinkling patterns, bright and bold,
Secrets shared and stories told.

Each shimmer dances in the dark,
A silent song, a gentle spark.
I trace the light, a twinkling line,
In night's embrace, our fates entwine.

Patterns woven from dreams' embrace,
Guiding hearts through endless space.
A cosmic rhythm, soft and sweet,
In the twinkle, we find our beat.

With every blink, a wish takes flight,
In a tapestry of purest light.
Together, we'll map the skies above,
In twinkling patterns, we find love.

## **Astral Needle's Dance**

With an astral needle, I sew,
Stitching dreams where starlight flows.
Each thread a wish upon the air,
A tapestry of love and care.

Across the night, the fabric streams,
In every corner, hope redeems.
The needle twirls, the cosmos spins,
In gentle arcs, where life begins.

A dance of light, a graceful glide,
In harmony, my heart's delight.
With stars as beads on fabric fine,
The needle's waltz, a tale divine.

In every stitch, a world unfolds,
With every twist, a dream retold.
In this celestial dance, I find,
An astral quilt, our hearts combined.

**Cosmic Embroidery**

Threads of starlight intertwined,
Patterns of the night aligned.
Galaxies in gentle sway,
Knit the fabric of the day.

A tapestry of dreams unfolds,
Whispers in the dark, retold.
Nebulae like vivid ink,
In space's vast canvas, we think.

Light-years weave the stories bright,
Crafted in the silent night.
A cosmic quilt of wonder spun,
Each stitch beneath the hidden sun.

Endless dance of time and space,
In this vast celestial place.
With every thread and twinkling star,
We find connections near and far.

## **Nightfall's Tapestry**

As dusk unfolds its velvet cloak,
Stars awaken, softly spoke.
Moonlight spills on tranquil seas,
Carefree whispers in the breeze.

Shadows play on whispered dreams,
Nighttime glimmers in moonbeams.
Constellations form their schemes,
In the stillness, hope redeems.

A soft embrace, the world slows down,
In silent grace, we wear night's crown.
The fabric of the dark divine,
Each thread of light a lifeline.

With every blink, more stories shared,
In cosmic layers gently bared.
Together we wander, lost and found,
In this tapestry, our hearts abound.

## Emblems of the Astral

Celestial symbols dance and glide,
In the void where dreams reside.
Pulsing lights in rhythmic flow,
Emblems of the unknown glow.

Each star a story, shining bright,
Guides us through the endless night.
Galactic maps of love and fear,
In the cosmos, we hold dear.

Orbs of color spin and twirl,
In this vast, enchanting whirl.
Mysteries wrapped in twilight's grace,
Emblems of life in boundless space.

A dance of shadows, bright and dark,
In the silence, we find our spark.
A journey through the astral seas,
With every star, our souls find ease.

## Whirling Nebulae and Twinkling Threads

In the cradle of the night sky,
Nebulae waltz, and comets fly.
Twinkling threads on cosmic winds,
Weaving tales where starlight blends.

Galaxies whirl in silent grace,
A dance of beauty in vast space.
Every shimmer, a whispered song,
Carried where the stars belong.

Through the darkness, colors bloom,
Painting secrets, dispelling gloom.
Life's connected by these beams,
Threads of light in cosmic dreams.

So we gaze up in wonder's thrall,
Feeling tiny, yet all in all.
In this dance of the endless night,
We find our place in the starlit light.

## Interstellar Fabrics

In the silent depths of space,
Threads of starlight softly trace,
Woven tales of time and light,
Binding realms of day and night.

Patterns born from cosmic sighs,
Galaxies in sparkling ties,
Every strand a whispered song,
In the fabric where we belong.

Nebulas with colors bright,
Dance beneath the velvet night,
Galactic hands knit tales anew,
Crafting dreams for me and you.

A tapestry of worlds unseen,
Stitched together in the serene,
Interstellar, vast and grand,
Held by love's eternal hand.

## **Celestial Weavecraft**

With dust of stars, the loom is spun,
Each thread a journey just begun,
Celestial beams cross and collide,
In the weavecraft where dreams abide.

Spotlights dance on cosmic seas,
Whispers drift on gentle breeze,
Weaving light, we traverse fate,
In the fabric of love, we wait.

Silk from comets, gold from suns,
Patterns bright where time outruns,
We spin with the moon, the sun,
In this craft, we are as one.

Embroidery of nights so deep,
In the cosmos, secrets keep,
Threads of hope and light converge,
In the weft and warp, we surge.

## **Cosmic Dreamscape**

In a dreamscape vast and wide,
Stars and planets gently glide,
Visions bloom in midnight's grace,
In the cosmic dream we chase.

Galaxies like whispers soar,
Pulsing deep in cosmic lore,
Every dream a starlit spark,
Guiding hearts through endless dark.

Nebulae in vibrant hue,
Echo songs of night and dew,
Within this cosmos, dreams align,
In the beauty, you are mine.

A tapestry of hopes and fears,
Woven through the silent years,
In this vast celestial dome,
We find meaning, we find home.

## **Night's Silken Yarns**

Night unfolds her silken threads,
Wrapping dreams in gentle spreads,
Moonlight paints the world in white,
Stitching shadows through the night.

Stars like beads on endless string,
Crafting peace that night can bring,
Each yarn a wish, a silent prayer,
In the stillness, soft and fair.

Whispers dance on midnight air,
Tales of love, dreams, and despair,
Yarns that weave the heart's delight,
In the fabric of the night.

Gentle winds through branches sway,
Carrying the dreams away,
In night's embrace, we find the balm,
Wrapping us in quiet calm.

**Hemming the Horizon**

The sun sinks low, a fiery crown,
Painting the sky in shades of brown.
Whispers of wind through grasses sway,
Hemming the edge of night and day.

Stars emerge, a twinkling show,
As twilight's curtain starts to grow.
Crickets sing their evening song,
A melody where we belong.

Clouds drift like dreams that softly float,
Carrying tales on a distant boat.
Horizon hems the world so wide,
As shadows dance where secrets hide.

**Night's Silken Weave**

In velvet dark, the stories weave,
Each star a thread, we do believe.
Moonlight spills on fields so fair,
Threads of silver in the air.

The night unfolds with a gentle hand,
A tapestry across the land.
Whispered hopes in silence gleam,
As dreams unravel, soft as cream.

Through the branches, shadows cast,
Moments cherished, memories fast.
The world transforms, a soft embrace,
In night's silken weave, we find our place.

# The Loom of Infinity

Time unfurls on a cosmic loom,
Weaving destinies amidst the gloom.
Threads of past and future blend,
In patterns that twist and bend.

Galaxies spin in endless dance,
Every moment, a fleeting chance.
Each choice a strand in fate's embrace,
A universal, timeless space.

Stars are knots in the fabric tight,
Holding secrets of day and night.
The loom of infinity extends so far,
Guiding souls like a wandering star.

## **Celestial Cross-Stitch**

In night's embrace, with needle fine,
We stitch the cosmos, line by line.
Each constellation, a crafted tale,
As dreams take flight on starlit trails.

Threads of gold and silver gleam,
Embroidering the fabric of dream.
Planets spin in a graceful thrust,
In the cross-stitch of cosmic trust.

With every knot, a wish is cast,
In the heaven's tapestry, vast.
Celestial patterns, bold and bright,
In this art of love, we find our light.

## **Embroidered Cosmic Dreams**

In the quiet of the night,
Stars twinkle in delight.
Threads of light intertwine,
Stitched in patterns so divine.

Galaxies spin like yarn,
Whispers of the cosmic dawn.
Nebulae in colors bright,
Weave the fabric of the night.

Each dream a silent prayer,
Softly floating through the air.
Minds adrift in endless space,
Finding peace in time and place.

Embroidered visions gleam,
In the heart, a waking dream.
Stitch by stitch, we dare to soar,
Crafting dreams forevermore.

## Crafting the Unseen

Beneath the veil of night,
Magic flows, a gentle light.
Hands that shape the unseen world,
As the mystic dust is twirled.

With each breath, we start to mold,
Stories waiting to be told.
Secrets hidden in the shade,
Crafting visions unafraid.

Silken threads of thought unite,
In the dark, they find their flight.
Woven into something bold,
Binding dreams in threads of gold.

Every heart a loom to weave,
Invisible ties we believe.
Creating realms where dreams take flight,
In the fabric of the night.

## The Weaving of Wishes

In the quiet of the stars,
Wishes whisper from afar.
Interlacing hopes and fears,
Crafted softly through the years.

Each intention, woven bright,
Threads of gold in silken night.
Tales of longing, soft and deep,
In the woven dreams we keep.

With each flicker, each desire,
Embers dance, igniting fire.
Stitches hold what hearts believe,
In the tapestry we weave.

Wishes scattered like the sand,
In the fabric, they make stand.
I close my eyes and dare to dream,
In the weave of life's grand scheme.

## An Astral Fabrication

In a realm where dreams reside,
Stars align, a cosmic guide.
Patterns form in silent grace,
An astral dance in boundless space.

Threads of fate, a tapestry,
Woven with the light we see.
Spirits soar on beams of light,
Crafting worlds beyond our sight.

Every stitch a tale untold,
Flying high, our hearts unfold.
In the night, we find our spark,
Applauding dreams that leave a mark.

With each heartbeat, we create,
Luminous paths, we navigate.
An astral world, vast and free,
In every fabric, you and me.

## The Thread of Eternity

In shadows where the silence dwells,
A whisper spins the timeless spells.
Each moment floats, a fleeting sigh,
A tapestry woven, bold and shy.

With colors bright and tales untold,
The fabric of our lives unfold.
In every stitch, a dream resides,
While love and loss, the thread abides.

The hands of time, they gently weave,
From joy to sorrow, we believe.
Eternity wraps us in its grace,
In this grand dance, we find our place.

A single thread can bind us all,
As echoes of our stories call.
We journey on, through dark and light,
In the thread of eternity, we unite.

## Cosmic Stitches

Stars adorn the vast expanse,
Each one a stitch in cosmic dance.
From galaxies to whispered dreams,
The universe flows, or so it seems.

Nebulas bloom in colors bright,
Woven gently into night.
A quilt of wonder, endless sky,
In each twinkling spark, a sigh.

Planets turn, in spirals they tread,
With gravitational threads they led.
The cosmos sings a lullaby,
Of endless journeys, far and nigh.

In darkness deep, the secrets lie,
Patterns of fate, they never die.
Through cosmic stitches, we explore,
The fabric of existence, forevermore.

## Patterns of the Night Sky

In the canvas where the darkness sprawls,
The night sky twinkles, softly calls.
Each star a note in silent song,
Guiding dreams where hearts belong.

Those argent patterns come alive,
In silver tapestries, hopes arrive.
Constellations whisper stories bold,
Of ancient times and futures foretold.

A crescent moon, a watchful eye,
Marks the hours as moments fly.
The starlit patterns weave our fate,
Inside the universe, we contemplate.

As comets blaze across the space,
The night holds secrets we embrace.
In patterns made of light so spry,
We find our truth beneath the sky.

## The Weave of Eons

In timeless threads where ancients tread,
The weft of eons softly spread.
With wisdom wrapped in every loop,
We sail through time, a wondrous troop.

Seasons spin in rhythmic grace,
As life unfolds in its embrace.
The past and future intertwine,
In the weave of eons, all align.

From dawn of worlds to twilight's rest,
Each moment penned, a sacred quest.
The fabric stretches, taut and free,
In patterns charting destiny.

With every breath, a story grows,
In colors blending, life bestows.
The weave of eons, strong and wide,
Holding the universe inside.

## Patchwork of Light

In the dawn's embrace, colors bloom,
Threads of gold, chasing away the gloom.
Fingers dance with a gentle grace,
Crafting tales in a sacred space.

Each square a story, layered and bright,
Fragments of dreams woven in light.
Stitched by hands that know the art,
Of binding together each fragile heart.

## Illuminated Stitches

Stitches sparkle like stars above,
Each knot a whisper, a promise of love.
Underneath the moon's soft glow,
Secrets of the night begin to flow.

Tapestries woven with hopes and fears,
Threads of laughter, threads of tears.
In every patch, a moment caught,
A glimpse of life, a lesson taught.

## Ethereal Sewings

In a realm where dreams take flight,
Sewing shadows into light.
Fibers dance on the edge of night,
Creating magic in each twilight.

With every stitch, the universe sings,
Binding together ethereal things.
Patterns emerge, a celestial guide,
Revealing wonders that stars confide.

## Woven Whispers of the Cosmos

Galaxies twirl in a night so deep,
Fingers weave secrets, gently they keep.
Threads of silence, a cosmic embrace,
Echoes of stardust, time and space.

Woven whispers float through the air,
An infinite tapestry, beyond compare.
Each stitch a heartbeat, a rhythm divine,
A dance of creation, eternally twine.

## Orbital Patterns and Cosmic Quilts

In the night sky, stars align,
Patterns woven, oh so fine.
Galaxies dance, a cosmic thread,
Mapping dreams where few have tread.

Each twinkle whispers tales untold,
In the vastness, bright and bold.
Celestial stitches, astral light,
Crafting wonders through the night.

Nebulas swirl in colors bright,
A tapestry of starry sight.
In every fold, a story spins,
Embracing all, where love begins.

Cosmic quilts of ages past,
Holding secrets, bound to last.
As we gaze, our hearts take flight,
In the wonder of the night.

# Starlit Fabrications

Under the blanket of the night,
Stars, like gems, spark pure delight.
Woven tales in the moon's glow,
Fabrications of space we know.

Constellations guide our dreams,
Each light a whisper, softly beams.
In the dark, our hopes take form,
Dancing gently through the storm.

Galactic threads pull us near,
In the silence, we hear the clear.
Stories crafted in time's embrace,
In the cosmos, we find our place.

With each gaze upon the skies,
We uncover life's sweet surprise.
Starlit fabrications unfold,
A treasure map for dreams untold.

## **Nebulae in Needlepoint**

Softly glowing, shadows collide,
Nebulae bloom where wonders hide.
With each stitch, a cosmos made,
In needlework, the stars arrayed.

Threads of color, vibrant hues,
Capturing light, a dance infused.
From every stitch, a story sewn,
In cosmic gardens, seeds are grown.

Whispers of gas, in layers spun,
Over millennia, light has run.
In every patch, a universe,
Crafted softly, a cosmic verse.

Needlepoint dreams in fabric vast,
Binding futures with the past.
In nebulae, our hopes we plant,
In starlit realms where spirits chant.

## **Lightwoven Fantasies**

With threads of light, we weave our dreams,
In the cosmos, reality beams.
From heart to star, each wish takes flight,
Lightwoven fantasies through the night.

Celestial patterns, bright and bold,
Stories of love, forever told.
In the fabric of the endless space,
We find solace, we find our place.

Galaxies spin, a gentle caress,
Each twinkle a promise, a soft caress.
In every glow, a memory pure,
Lightwoven tales that long endure.

With every dream, a new design,
In the tapestry where hearts entwine.
Woven in starlight, sharing our song,
In the fabric of night, we all belong.

## The Sewing of Shadows

In twilight's quilt, the shadows weave,
Whispers of dreams the night believes.
With needle fine, they stitch the light,
Crafting tales in silent night.

A tapestry of hopes and fears,
Woven deep with quiet sears.
The fabric holds our secret sighs,
Underneath the starlit skies.

Each thread a story, each knot a tale,
Bound by fate, they shall not pale.
In shadow's embrace, we find our thread,
A new dawn dawns, where none shall dread.

So let us sew beneath the moon,
Where shadows dance and dreams are strewn.
In every stitch, a heart's refrain,
Together we shall weave the pain.

## **Daydreams in the Dark**

In the stillness, whispers sigh,
Casting visions up to the sky.
Daydreams play in silent night,
Filling souls with pure delight.

Imagined lands where spirits soar,
Awake the dreams we can't ignore.
In shadows, we find our flight,
Chasing stars, igniting light.

With every thought, the darkness bends,
Creating paths where magic lends.
In the quiet, minds are stark,
Blooming daydreams in the dark.

Close your eyes, let dreams impart,
Whispered secrets to the heart.
In the night, let visions spark,
Life's bright canvas, paint the dark.

# Threads of the Cosmos

In cosmic dance, the threads align,
Weaving stars in endless design.
Galaxies spin on celestial looms,
Crafting wonders that brightly bloom.

Each thread a tale from ancient time,
In harmony, they sing and chime.
A tapestry of light and dark,
In every stitch, the universe sparks.

From nebulae to distant shores,
The cosmos hums with distant roars.
Binding time with space in grace,
In every thread, we find our place.

So dance within this cosmic seas,
Embrace the wonders with gentle ease.
Threads of fate that bind us tight,
In the fabric of endless light.

## Night's Radiant Weave

Beneath the veil of midnight's glow,
Stars emerge in a radiant row.
Threads of silver, softly spun,
Embrace the dreams, the day is done.

With every glance, the heart does swell,
In night's embrace, all is well.
Patterns form in quiet grace,
A gentle weave where shadows chase.

From dusk till dawn, the stories flow,
In velvet skies, the secrets grow.
A tapestry of love and fear,
In the night's embrace, we hold dear.

So let us dance under the stars,
Celebrate the night, forget our scars.
In night's radiant weave, we find,
The beauty of a boundless mind.

## Constellation Needlework

In the darkness, patterns gleam,
Stars like stitches, in a dream.
Sewn with care, by hands unseen,
A tapestry of night's serene.

Whispers of time in the sky,
Guiding seekers, drawing nigh.
Each twinkle tells a hidden tale,
Of journeys past, of winds that sail.

Soft threads of light, they intertwine,
Map of souls, it's so divine.
Patterns shift with every breath,
Crafted whispers, life and death.

In the cosmos, we find our place,
Sewing dreams in endless space.
Needles that pierce the blackened sky,
Keeping secrets, fluttering high.

## Threads of the Universe

Strings of starlight cross the void,
Woven whispers, never coy.
Each delicate thread tells a story,
Of celestial dance and ancient glory.

Galaxies spin in cosmic flow,
Threads that shimmer, ebb and glow.
Binding time in threads of grace,
A fabric woven with pure embrace.

In each stitch, a dream unfurls,
Crafting unity through distant worlds.
Intertwined in cosmic fate,
A tapestry, we celebrate.

The universe, a loom of light,
Weaving wonders, day and night.
Eternal threads that never fray,
Binding hearts in cosmic play.

**Cosmic Fabric**

In the void where silence reigns,
Cosmic fabric, soft as rains.
Quilts of stars, a night's embrace,
Patterns shift, celestial grace.

Stitches pull the heavens tight,
Crafting shadows, embracing light.
Each galaxy, a seam of time,
Rhythms pulse in perfect rhyme.

Nebulas bloom like flowers bright,
Colors weaving, pure delight.
Each moment captured, each love sewn,
In this fabric, we are grown.

Eternal fabric, we reside,
In its embrace, stars collide.
Bound by threads of fate so grand,
We journey through this vast expanse.

## **Luminous Stitches**

Luminous stitches light the sky,
Embroidering tales that never die.
With every thread, a wish takes flight,
Painting dreams in the cosmic night.

Each dotted star, a promise made,
Weaving hopes, never to fade.
Patterns of love that dance and sing,
In cosmic circles, endlessly ring.

Sewn with laughter, threaded with tears,
Filling the heavens, calming our fears.
Each shimmering stitch a guiding light,
Leading us home through the endless night.

In this quilt of the universe,
We find our place, we're never terse.
With luminous stitches, we explore,
The wonders of space, forevermore.

# **Glittering Woven Tales**

In the loom of time, we thread our dreams,
Stitching moments, unraveling seams.
Each tale glimmers, a star in the night,
Woven with whispers, holding the light.

Colors and patterns, they dance in the air,
Each strand a story, a love laid bare.
From fabric of memories, we sew and bind,
In the tapestry of life, our hearts aligned.

Ribbons of laughter entwine with our tears,
Every knot echoes the passage of years.
In the gallery of souls, our stories reside,
A quilt of existence, where hopes collide.

Glittering woven tales shall endure,
In the hearts of the dreamers, ever pure.
With threads of gold and shadows that play,
We craft our legacy, come what may.

**Sewing the Night**

Underneath the stars, we gather and sew,
Stitching the darkness, letting time flow.
Needles of silver, they glide through the bliss,
Mending the seams with each hopeful kiss.

The moonlight guides our delicate thread,
Whispers of dreams in the silence spread.
We patch up the shadows that softly creep,
Sewing the night, where secrets sleep.

With every stitch, we conquer the fears,
Filling the fabric with laughter and tears.
The tapestry grows, a mosaic of fate,
Sewing the night, where we cultivate.

In the warmth of starlight, our stories intertwine,
Each stitch a promise, entwined like a vine.
As dawn breaks softly, we'll cherish the light,
For we stitched together the beautiful night.

## Nebula Patterns

Patterns of starlight in the cosmic quilt,
Nebulae dance where galaxies are built.
Colors swirling in the velvet expanse,
Creating a map where the wonders prance.

Threads of time weave through the vast unknown,
Each pattern a story, each star a tone.
Celestial fabric, with luminous swirls,
Crafting the cosmos, where mystery unfurls.

Captured in orbs of shimmering bright,
Nebula patterns whisper secrets of light.
Connecting the dots of the universe grand,
Crafting our fate with a delicate hand.

In the canvas of dark, the brilliance reveals,
Nebulae sing of the dreams that it heals.
A universe stitched with a love intertwined,
Holding the secrets that light up the mind.

## **Threads of Stardust**

Threads of stardust drift through the air,
Whispers of cosmos, fleeting and rare.
Each glimmering piece, a wish on the breeze,
Binding our lives with a gentle tease.

Woven through stories of old and new,
A tapestry shimmering in vibrant hue.
Each thread a moment, a memory bright,
Sewn into fabric, illuminating the night.

From distant dreams where time doesn't wane,
Threads of stardust dance through joy and pain.
In the loom of existence, we spin and sway,
Crafting our journeys in a poetic ballet.

So let us embrace this celestial art,
Threads of stardust flowing from heart to heart.
In the cosmos' embrace, we are never apart,
For the universe sings through each beating heart.

Milton Keynes UK
Ingram Content Group UK Ltd.
UKHW021913201124
451474UK00013B/733